99 Ant Jokes

by Toby & Rafe Menon

Introduction

Three years ago, our Grandpa Kurt started telling us jokes he called "ant jokes". These were jokes in which the punch line contained the word ant, such as "What do you call an ant that likes rolling places? A Tyrant!" In this case Tyrant would be Tire-ant, to describe the rolling. We found these jokes exceptionally funny, and began coming up with our own. This book is a collection of the funniest, craziest, and most outrageous ant jokes that we, along with our Grandpa Kurt and Grandma Sheila, have come up with.

-Toby and Rafe Menon
March 2017

Printed in the United States of America
First Printing, 2017
ISBN 978-1543297379
Scribord House, an imprint of Writing It Real
394 Colman Drive
Port Townsend, WA 98368
www.writingitreal.com

1. What do you call an ant
that is obsessed with
vulcanized rubber?

A Tyrant!

2. What do you call ants
that go all over?

Romance!

3. What do ants do when the music starts?

Dance!

4. What do you call an ant that sells goods from other countries?

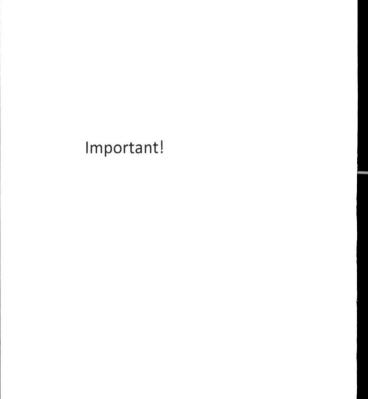

Important!

5. What do you call an ant that is unable to do anything?

A Can't!

6. What do you call an ant that competes a lot?

A Contestant!

7. What do you call an ant that is always included?

A Participant!

8. What do you call the foolish behavior of an ant?

Antics!

9. What do you call an ant
that writes cookbooks?

A Recipient!

10. What do you call a
baby ant?

An Infant!

11. What do you call
someone who hurts ants?

An Antagonizer!

12. Where do you send a disrespectful young ant?

Antwerp!

13. Why do ants get excited?

From Anticipation!

14. What does an ant do
when it is mad?

It Rants!

15. What do you call a gala for really big ants?

One-Inch-Anted Evening!

16. What do ants call
humans?

Giants!

17. What is it called when an ant doesn't reach home with the food it is carrying?

An Anticlimax!

18. What type of ant rides reindeer?

Santa!

19. What type of reindeer are they?

Ones with Antlers!

20. And what does Santa give the other ants?

Presents!

21. Where do English ants live?

Canterbury!

22. What do ants call refrigerators?

Antarctica!

23. What do you call two opposing ants?

Antonyms!

24. What do you call an
ant that carries a candy
dispenser everywhere?

A Peasant!

25. What kind of ant glows?

A Radiant!

26. What do you call an ant that learns by osmosis?

Absorbent!

27. What do you call a small number of ants?

Scant!

28. What kind of ant lives between mountains?

Valiant!

29. What kind of ants look
at things briefly?

Glance!

30. What is an ant in relation to its great grandfather?

A Descendant!

31. What do you call an ant's father's sister?

Its Aunt!

32. What do you call a
self-appointed police ant?

Vigilante!

33. What kind of ant is at the top of a mountain?

Piquant!

34. What do you call an ant that is always sticking its tongue out at others?

Flagrant!

35. What do you call an ant that's uncooperative?

Defiant!

36. What do you call an ant that smells good?

Fragrant!

37. What do you call a ten-year-old ant?

Decadent!

38. What do you call an ant
that cleans up smells?

Deodorant!

39. What do you call ants lined up two by two?

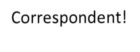

Correspondent!

40. Why did the ant buckle his seatbelt?

Because the Attendant
said there was
Turbulence!

41. What do you call an ant that lives between two bushes?

A Transplant!

42. Which ant do you call
on to answer a question?

A Respondent!

43. What kind of ant
leaves out the vowels?

A Consonant!

44. What do you call an ant in Harry Potter?

Fantasized!

45. What do you call the
best of the ants?

Brilliant!

46. What do you call an
ant that defies gravity?

Ascendant!

47. What do you call an ant with ESP?

An Expectorant!

48. What do you call an ant who is always spacing out?

Vacant!

49. What kind of ant used to be fast?

An Expedient!

50. What do you call an
ant that likes pasta?

Mac ant Cheese!

51. What do you call an
ant you can't park next to?

A Fire Hydrant!

52. What do you call an
ant in the garden?

A Plant!

53. What do you call an
ant that panics a lot?

Frantic!

54. What do you call an ant that can fly?

A Pheasant!

55. What do you call an
ant who drives a car?

A Rodent!

56. What do you call an ant with a degree in English?

Semantic!

57. What do you call an
ant bigger than a giant?

Gigantic!

58. What do you call a tilted ant?

A Slant!

59. What do ants do to
psych themselves up?

Chant!

60. What do you call an ant that is fun to be around?

Pleasant!

61. What do you call an
ant that swims in schools?

An Anchovy!

62. What do you call an
ant that can do magic?

An Enchantress!

63. What do you call an ant that helps people with their money?

A Financial Agent!

64. What do you call a supervising ant?

A Commandant!

65. What does a tired ant do?

It Pants!

66. What do you call 200 ants trying to move a boulder?

Insufficient!

67. What do you call an ant that can't move a crumb?

Incompetent!

68. What kind of ant lights
up your room?

A Fluorescent!

69. What do you call an
ant that does gymnastics?

Flippant!

70. What do you call an ant that's just been insulted?

Distant!

71. What do you call an
ant that you trust?

An Antitrust!

72. What do you call an
ant that is sticky from sap?

Resonant!

73. What do you call a young male ant?

Buoyant!

74. What do you call an
ant that can't talk?

Mutant!

75. What do you call an
ant that says things twice?

Redundant!

76. What do you call an ant with a sequined gown?

Obedient!

77. What do you call an ant who goes to a groom's party?

Stagnant!

78. What do you call an old ant?

Antique!

79. What is an ant's favorite finger?

His Anthem!

80. What do you call an
ant that lives at college?

Dormant!

81. What do you call an ant that hides in doorways?

An Endorsement!

82. Which ant is good at basketball?

Kevin Durant!

83. What kind of ant tells on other ants?

An Informant!

84. What is in a 1000 ant
army?

Militants!

85. What do you call an
ant that tastes disgusting?

Violent!

86. What do you call a group of ants that brews potions?

Covenant!

87. What do you call a
young ant's big brother?

Tolerant!

88. What do you call a
female ant?

Gallant!

89. What do you call ants that sell protection to other ants?

Insurance!

90. What nickname does
Louis Fredrick Ant go by
based on his initials?

Elephant!

91. What do you call ants
that hang out by ruins?

Remnants!

92. What do you call an
ant that always wins?

Triumphant!

93. What do you call it when two ants run off to get married?

An Antelope!

94. What do you call an ant on bedrest for a week with a bad cough?

Affluent!

95. What do you call an ant who never lies?

A Truant!

96. What do you call an ant who is a stickler for boring detail?

Pedantic!

97. What do you call an ant that looks just like his friends?

Congruent!

98. What do you call an ant that you can feel but never see?

A Phantom!

99. What do you call a small ant?

An ant!

56102666R00124

Made in the USA
San Bernardino, CA
10 November 2017